Paper Crafts

31 Awesome Crafts You'll Love to Make!

Read This FIRST - 100% FREE BONUS

Check Out Kitty's Free Giveaway!

FOR A LIMITED TIME ONLY – Get Kitty's Best Selling book *"100 Ultimate Crafts For A Rainy Day"* absolutely FREE!

<u>CLICK HERE to download YOUR free copy!</u>

Readers who have read the bonus book along with this book have seen the greatest changes in their crafting abilities and have expanded their repertoire of crafts– so it is *highly recommended* to get this bonus book.

Once again, as a big thank-you for downloading this book, I'd like to offer it to you 100% FREE for a LIMITED TIME ONLY!

<u>CLICK HERE to download YOUR free copy!</u>

For IMAGES of the final product of each of the crafts in this book CLICK on this link

CLICK here for instant access to image gallery!

Other Books By Kitty Moore

Table of Contents

Introduction

Looking for something to while away the afternoon? Or do you need a little extra oomph at your next party? Paper crafts are relatively inexpensive – you can even choose to recycle materials if you want – and all you really need is some creativity, a few pieces of paper, scissors and glue.

Let your creativity loose and you will find that you will never be short of personalized greeting cards and small gifts again.

And you get to decide how much time and energy you want to put into things – the paper craft projects in this book will spur your imagination and help you to learn skills that you can apply in projects of your own design.

I love paper crafting – there are infinite design opportunities and so many different tools and techniques that one can use. You never need to worry about being bored again. Whether you want to make projects to keep all to yourself or want to use paper craft as an overall means of expression, you are going to find something to keep you occupied.

And you don't need to worry about having all the fancy, expensive tools either – you can build up your collection as you go along. Just as an example, I finally bought a bone folder a few months ago but hardly ever use it – the back of a spoon works just as well!

That said, you will need to have a good ruler and sharp pair of scissors. If this is something that takes your fancy, I do advise investing in a paper trimmer – it really makes short work cutting strips and creating a much more professional looking finish.

You can find tons of free printable papers and templates online and I advise downloading some of these to practice on before you buy the more expensive card stock and scrap-booking papers in the store.

As far as adhesives go, consider the project you will be making first – I use the acid-free adhesive for projects that are intended to be keepsakes, but I stick to a regular old stick of glue for basic party decorations and the like – if I am going to get sick of something and bin it in a few months time, I don't spend a fortune on suppliers. If I am making a gift for the grandparents, I put a bit more effort into it.

Happy crafting!

Pretty Card and Envelope

Materials

- Card stock – double the size of your envelope – it should fit snugly when inserted
- Bone folder or a dinner spoon and butter knife
- An envelope to use as a template
- Paper cutter
- Pencil
- Paper scissors – if you want to, use those with a serrated edge
- Images that you like – out of a magazine or downloaded
- Pretty paper – this project is ideal for using up those scraps
- Glue stick

Directions

1. Measure your envelope and trim the card stock so that it will fit into it properly. Fold the card in half and lightly mark the mid-point on both edges of the card.

2. Take your ruler and line it up with the marks that you made. Hold the ruler firmly down and run the pointed end of your bone folder or the tip of the butter knife along the line, using the ruler as a guide, to lightly score the paper.

3. Fold the card along the crease and run the blunt edge of the bone folder or the back of the spoon over the fold to flatten it out.

4. Arrange the pictures you have chosen on the front of the card to make a nice collage of images and glue them down.

5. You can also cut some scraps of paper into interesting shapes and glue these on.

6. Set aside to dry.

7. Carefully open out the envelope so that you can use it as a template, noting how it was originally folded. Steaming can release the adhesive in need. Get a clean piece of plain paper and trace the outline of the envelope onto it.

8. Cut the shape out.

9. Score the envelope shape lightly along the fold lines.

10. Cut a piece of paper/ images matching your card so that it fits into the inside top flap of the envelope and glue it down.

11. Fold the envelope, securing all but the closing flap with glue.

Make Your Own Tags

Materials

- Glue stick

- Heavy-weight paper

- Pencil

- Paper scissors

- Yarn, string or thin ribbon

- Ruler

- Cookie cutters

- Embellishments like sequins, flowers, etc

- Punch

Directions

1. Choose paper that appeals to you – it should relatively sturdy.

2. Trace the outline of your cookie cutters onto the paper.

3. Cut out neatly and punch a hole into the paper so that you can tie the string on.

4. Glue on the embellishments that you prefer – use your creativity here – look for things that will add extra dimensions and textures – bits and pieces of a lace doily, for example. Do leave one side blank for writing on.

5. Tie on the ribbon or yarn and your tag is ready to use.

Quick And Easy Gift Wrap

Materials

- A roll of brown paper
- Spray paint in two colors of your choice – metallic paints work nicely
- Images or letters you can use as a negative for the main picture
- Different items to use to create different background patterns – paper doilies, pieces of the netting used for vegetables, etc.

Directions

1. Spread out the paper onto a flat surface – put newspaper down first so that there is less mess.

2. Arrange the items you are using for the background and lay them flat on the paper.

3. Spray over the whole paper with your first color spray paint – concentrate on some areas more than others to make the background nice and varied.

4. Leave to dry for about 20 minutes and remove the items chosen for the background.

5. Arrange the images or letters for the main picture and repeat steps 3 and 4.

Paper Pumpkins

Materials

- Construction paper in green and orange
- Glue
- Scissors
- Round cookie cutter
- Pencil

Directions

1. Trace a circle on your orange paper in order using the cookie cutter as a template. Make 10 such circles and trim carefully.

2. Fold each of the circles but one first in half and then into quarters.

3. Unfold each of the quarter circles. Using this fold line as a guide, with the remaining folded side on the left, cut a slit that stops short of the edge by about 3/8 inches.

4. Set aside and using green paper, cut out a rectangle ½ wide and about double the diameter of the circles that you cut. Fold in half along the longest edge.

5. Fold one end of the rectangle a little so that you use this as a tab. Glue this to the middle of the one unfolded circle.

6. Now finish off by aligning the slits of each folded circle and sliding them onto the circle that you did not fold. Arrange so that it looks more like a pumpkin.

Luxurious Gift Bag

Materials

- Patterned, heavy paper
- Stamps of your choice
- Embellishments
- Glue
- Buttons
- Paper doilies

Directions

1. Fold the patterned paper in half and turn up the edges so that you have a basic gift bag. Glue edges.

2. Position the doily on the front of the bag, trimming if necessary. Glue into place.

3. Cut a strip from a coordinating piece of patterned paper – it must be wide enough to cover the plain center of the doily and the same length as your bag. Glue onto the center of the doily.

4. Decorate this strip with buttons or the embellishments of your choice – use a hot glue gun to stick heavier pieces in place. This is where you can be creative.

Toilet Roll Flowers

Materials

- A few empty toilet paper rolls
- Glue
- Paint
- A sharp craft knife
- Ruler
- Pencil

Directions

1. Using your ruler, mark out 1/4 inch sections of the toilet rolls.

2. Using your craft knife, cut along these lines so that you have several pieces smaller tubes. These will be your petals.

3. Flatten each tube slightly so they look more like petals.

4. Each flower has 5 petals. (You can make more if you like, but this should always be an odd number).

5. Arrange each of the petals individually – placing the inner corners together so that you get a flower shape. When happy with the design, glue together.

6. Paint if desired.

Scrap Happy Flowers

Materials

- Scrap paper and card
- Mod podge
- Stickers, embellishments and buttons
- Foam brush
- Scissors
- Hot glue gun
- Stick glue

Directions

1. Start off by cutting a circle out of card.
2. Cut petal shapes out of scraps of paper.
3. Cover each petal with a layer of ModgePodge allow to dry.
4. Glue each petal onto your circle, covering the card completely and paint front and back with ModgePodge. Leave to dry.
5. Add stickers to embellish petals.
6. Cut a small circle out of card to form the center of the flower.
7. Glue on top of the petals and apply another layer of ModgePodge.
8. Choose either an embellishment or button to go in the center of the flower.
9. Glue in place with the hot glue gun.

Paper Mache Bowl

Materials

- Water
- Elmer's glue
- Old plastic container
- Balloon
- Newspaper
- Foam brushes
- Disposable cup
- Gesso
- Paint
- String

Directions

1. Mix one part water to two parts glue and stir well.

2. Shred newspaper and let it soak in the glue mixture.

3. Cover one half of the balloon with these soaked strips and build up a good few layers.

4. Balance uncovered bit of balloon on cup and leave to dry overnight.

5. Paint with gesso and leave to dry.

6. Pop the balloon.

7. Paint the inside with gesso and leave to dry.

8. Make pretty shapes on the outside of the bowl using string. When happy, glue it into place.

9. Once this is dry, paint the inside and outside of the bowl.

Toilet Roll Gift Tube

Materials

- Toilet rolls
- Scraps of patterned paper and ribbon
- Embellishments

Directions

1. Cut paper to fit around toilet tube and glue on.

2. Insert the gift.

3. Fold each end of the tube carefully about a ¼ of an inch from the edge so that the holes at either end of the tube close properly. You can glue one edge to the other for greater stability.

4. Decorate the tube using ribbon and scrap paper.

Mini-Journal

Materials

- Plain card stock
- Construction paper
- Patterned paper
- Protractor
- Tapestry needle
- Ruler
- Yarn

Directions

1. Fold your card stock in half and flatten the fold using the back of a spoon or a bone folder.

2. Open out and lay construction paper on top. The cover should be a ¼ inch bigger than the construction paper pages.

3. Fold the construction paper in half.

4. Measure to locate the exact center on both the cover and the pages.

5. Make a hole all the way through using the protractor.

6. Make a second hole about 1 inch from the top of the page and a third hole 1 inch from the bottom of the page.

7. Thread the needle using yarn and make running stitches between the holes so that all the pages are secure. Knot the end of the yarn, ending inside the book.

Paper Beads

Materials

- Ruler
- A4 sheet of paper – plain or patterned, magazine pages work well
- Scissors
- Strong glue
- Toothpicks
- Pencil
- Clear nail varnish
- String
- Dish cleaning sponge

Directions

1. Mark off 1.5 cm increments on the short edge of you paper. On the opposite edge, mark off increments of 1 cm.

2. Cut the triangles out.

3. Pick up a toothpick and, starting at the widest edge of the skewer, start rolling the paper tightly onto it until only a small edge is left.

4. Glue the tip to the body of the bead.

5. Apply a coat of nail varnish.

6. Stick toothpick into the piece of foam so that the bead is not touching anything and leave to dry.

Paper Mosaic

Materials

- Elmer's glue
- Poster board
- Pencil
- Scrap paper
- Picture to use as a template
- Ruler
- Scissors or square punch
- Clear varnish

Directions

1. Cut or punch your paper into small squares. They do not have to be perfect.

2. Transfer your picture onto the poster board.

3. Start filling in the picture using the appropriate colored squares. You will build the picture in the same way as you would when using mosaic tiles. Glue each square into place.

4. Leave to dry and apply a coat of clear varnish.

Recycled Magazine Bowl

Materials

- Old magazines
- Elmer's glue
- Scissors or paper trimmer
- Modgepodge
- A sponge brush

Directions

1. Find colorful pages in the magazines – you will need around 25 of them. Tear out and neaten the edges with the paper trimmer/ scissors.

2. Fold each page in half and cut along the fold.

3. Fold each half into a strip – the end result should be about a ¼ inch wide.

4. Glue the edges down.

5. Now start pushing the end of each strip into the next one so that you end up with a long "rope".

6. Make a firm base by coiling the "rope" in a spiral and glue the layers as you go along.

7. When your base is big enough, start building up the basket. Each subsequent layer of "rope" should be anchored at about halfway up the previous layers.

8. Apply ModgePodge to the inside and outside of the bowl to seal it.

Simple Wall Art

Materials

- Patterned paper to match your décor
- An old box-mounted canvas or a flat frame without the glass
- Spray-on adhesive
- Modgepodge

Directions

1. Cut the paper to the same size as your canvas or frame.

2. Glue down using spray adhesive working slowly to ensure that there are no bubbles.

3. Apply ModgePodge to seal.

Paper Bunting

Materials

- Paper scraps
- String or yarn
- Glue
- Scissors

Directions

1. The size of the bunting will depend on what you are using it for. It should be fairly evenly placed across the string so choose a size that suits your purpose.

2. Cut simple diamond shapes from the paper.

3. You can punch the edges to get a more interesting finish if you like.

4. Arrange the diamonds along the string to get the color pattern and finish that you like.

5. When satisfied, fold each of the diamonds in half, enclosing the string along the fold.

6. Glue all the edges together.

Paper Yo-Yo

Materials

- Scraps of plain or patterned paper
- Plain card
- Buttons
- Hot glue gun
- Stick glue

Directions

1. Cut squares out of your scraps of paper – the bigger the square, the bigger the embellishment will be.

2. Fold each square lengthways so that you get an accordion effect.

3. Pinch one end of the "accordion" together and glue in place.

4. Take another "accordion" and place it next to the first, pinched ends together.

5. Glue the end strips that are now back to back.

6. Open out the resulting "accordion" and see if the end strips that have now been left open can be joined whilst still maintaining the effect.

7. If so, glue them together, if not, repeat steps 4-6 until the desired effect is achieved.

8. Cut two circles of card smaller than the diameter of the "accordion" and glue them in place with the hot glue gun. This will help create a stable base.

9. Stick pretty buttons onto the front to finish off.

Rose Wrapping Paper

Materials

- Bunch of celery
- Plain paper – A3 size
- Acrylic paints or ink
- A flat dish
- String

Directions

1. Using a sharp knife, cut the celery around about two inches from its base.

2. The base is going to be your stamp.

3. Tie the string loosely around the base.

4. Add the paint or ink to a flat dish. The acrylics should be easy flow acrylics.

5. Dip the cut end of the celery into the paint/ ink and stamp a design onto the paper.

6. Repeat until you get the effect that you want.

Faux Quill Flower

Materials

- 1 sheet of A4 paper
- Glue
- Paper trimmer or scissors
- Pearl bead for center

Directions

1. Cut the paper into equal sized strips running across the width of the paper.

2. Set aside half the strips.

3. Cut about an inch off the ends of half of the remaining strips.

4. Fold these strips in half loosely to form petals. Glue the ends of the strips together.

5. Glue the slightly longer strips onto the outside of these strips so that you have a petal enclosing a second petal. Glue the edges down.

6. Repeat with the remaining strips, trimming if need be. You should now have a petal within two petals.

7. Glue all the bottom ends of the petals together.

8. Glue the pearl into the center.

Votive Shades

Materials

- Votive candles in glass containers
- Plain white paper
- Oil
- Scissors
- Acrylic paints
- Glue
- Craft border punch (optional)

Directions

1. Measure the circumference of your votive candle.

2. Add 5 inches and cut the paper to match in terms of length.

3. You can choose to either paint a design on the paper or stick to bands of color using the paints. Clear, bright colors work best.

4. Leave to dry.

5. Turn the page over and soak some cotton wool in the oil.

6. Rub the cotton wool slowly over the back of the paper.

7. This will make the paper more translucent.

8. Punch the border of one edge if you like.

9. Roll the paper so that the art faces outwards and glue edges together.

10. Place around the votive candle, making sure that no edges are too near the flame.

Coffee Filter Roses

Materials

- Coffee filters
- Watercolor paints
- Spray bottle
- Scissors
- Hot glue gun
- Florist stems
- Florist tape

Directions

1. Cut the coffee filter into a rough spiral shape.
2. Starting with the outer edge of the spiral, roll to make your rose center.
3. Continue rolling the filter, making it looser towards the outer edge.
4. If you want a fuller flower, add more filters.
5. Place a dollop of hot glue at the base of the petals to keep them in place.
6. While the glue is still warm, push the florist stem into it.
7. When the glue has dried, wrap the bottom edge of the rose with the florist's tape.
8. Mix a weak wash of water color in the color you want and sprits it onto the rose, concentrating more color in the center.

Yarn Silhouette For A Kid's Room

Materials

- Two pieces of A4 plain white paper
- Image of your choice – choose a simple silhouette
- Yarn or ribbon in different colors
- Glue
- Frame

Directions

1. Print out a template which appeals to you on both pages.

2. Cut the shape out of one page so that you are left with the negative silhouette.

3. Cut the yarn or ribbon into strips that are just wide enough to cover the silhouette.

4. Lay the strips out in a pattern that you like over the printed page that you did not cut – you want to block out the picture altogether.

5. When happy tape the strips in place and place the cut negative over the top.

6. Glue into place and frame when dry.

Easy Envelope

Materials

- Scrap paper or card
- Ribbon
- Glue
- A round cookie cutter or glass

Directions

1. Trace four circles onto your paper and cut out carefully.

2. Fold each circle in half and open out again.

3. Lay the first circle on the table.

4. The second circle is placed next to this one, with the bottom halves overlapping.

5. Slot the third circle in between the first two, making sure that only the bottom half overlaps again.

6. Do the same for the fourth circle.

7. The circles should overlap enough that there are no gaps in the base.

8. Glue together.

9. Fold in the outer edges and you have an envelope.

10. Use ribbon to decorate and seal.

Heart Mobile

Materials

- Patterned paper
- Scissors
- Glue
- Punch
- Yarn or string

Directions

1. Cut four heart shapes out of the patterned paper.

2. Fold each in half.

3. Place two hearts together, wrong sides facing each other and lining up half of each heart.

4. Glue those halves together. You will now glue the next heart onto the other side of the first, wrong sides facing.

5. Repeat with the remaining two hearts.

6. Punch a hole in the top and string up with yarn or string.

Woven Magazine Coasters

Materials

- Old magazines
- Paper trimmer or scissors
- ModgePodge
- Glue

Directions

1. Each coaster will require 6 pages. Trim the pages to neaten them off.

2. Cut in half lengthwise or, if you want a finer look, cut into quarters.

3. Each strip should be folded in half again – lengthwise. Fold these halves in thirds and make sure that no cut edges show.

4. Now fold these strips in half across their width.

5. You should now be able to interlock the strips. Start with two interlocked at right angles to one another to form the first corner.

6. Add in your next strip so that is next to the corner.

7. Place the next strip at right angles to this one and start weaving the ends together.

8. Continue in this manner until all the strips are used, making sure that there are few gaps.

9. Trim any strips that peak over the edges, leaving just enough room to tuck them in underneath.

10. Glue the end strips down.

11. Seal with a few layers of ModgePodge.

Easy Decoration For Drinks

Materials

- Patterned paper or card
- Punch
- Bendy straws
- Flower template (or a shape of your choice)
- Scissors
- Glue

Directions

1. Find a flower template online and download it. Print onto your sheet of paper.
2. Cut each flower out individually.
3. Cut a circle out of contrasting paper to form the center of the flower.
4. Glue it down.
5. Punch a hole through the center of the flower and insert the straw.
6. Use the straw to liven up your drinks.

Easy Watercolor Wall Art

Materials

- Water color paints of your choosing
- Bubble blowing ring
- Water
- Dish washing liquid
- Water color paper
- Disposable cups

Directions

1. Mix up a teaspoon of dishwashing liquid into a liter or water.

2. Choose the colors that you want to use and assign a cup for each color.

3. Add a bit of the water mix into each cup and then add the color of your choice.

4. Mix well but stir slowly so that there are not too many bubbles.

5. Place your paper on the table.

6. Blow bubbles in the color of your choice so that they land on the paper. When they pop, they will leave behind interesting colors and textures.

Elegant Paper Christmas Tree

Materials

- Paper in the colors of your choice
- A thick piece of card for the base
- A skewer
- Glue
- Glitter
- Scissors with a serrated edge
- A bead big enough to fit on skewer

Directions

1. Push the skewer through the center of the thick card and glue into place.

2. Cut up sheets of paper into squares – you will need a lot – using the serrated scissors.

3. The first layer will be the biggest and will form the base. Make sure that it is big enough to cover the card base.

4. Skewer one of the papers cut and then add the next one at a slightly different degree.

5. You are going to build up your papers in a spiral format. As soon as you have finished a round in the first size, make the next block a little smaller and continue until your tree tapers to a tiny piece of paper.

6. Thread the bead onto the skewer and glue into place.

7. Sprinkle glitter over the tree.

Cookie Tin Memo Board

Materials

- A cookie tin
- Patterned papers in coordinating colors
- Glue
- Modgepodge
- Acrylic paint

Directions

1. Clean the cookie tin and brush a layer of ModgePodge over the surface.

2. Once this has dried, paint it.

3. Cut the paper in different sized strips no bigger than the cookie tin.

4. Arrange the strips as you like and then glue into place.

5. If you have a craft punch, you can also add punched flowers or shapes.

6. Cover everything with a layer of ModgePodge.

Bird's Nest Bowl

Materials

- 4 sheets of heavy weight paper per bowl
- Scissors
- Shredder (optional)
- Elmer's glue
- Water
- Nesting bowls
- Cling wrap
- Brush

Directions

1. Shred the paper or cut it up with scissors.
2. Mix two parts glue to one part water.
3. Turn the bowls upside down and put the cling wrap over the outside.
4. Dampen the paper slightly and then paint glue onto a small piece of the glue.
5. Apply the strips working slowly until they are all in place and held together.
6. Let the first layer dry before applying the second layer.
7. Once that is dry apply one more layer and finish off with a coat of glue.
8. Leave to dry in a warm sunny place.

Huge Paper Flowers

Materials

- Crepe paper – in green and a color of your choice
- A large heart template – download or draw it – it should be A4 size at least
- Glue
- A leaf template
- Wire – fairly thick, it needs to hold flower up
- Florists tape
- Scissors

Directions

1. Cut out 32 petals using your heart template and 8 leaves using your leaf template.

2. Roll the first petal to form the center of the rose and curl the outer edge of the petal slightly.

3. Add petals as you go along, shaping them to look more realistic. Glue in place as you go.

4. When you are done, cover your wire with florist's tape and slide into the base of the rose.

5. Glue the leaves onto the outside of the base of the rose so that it is completely covered.

6. Wrap florist's wire around the base to secure it.

Easy Butterfly Wall Art

Materials

- Large butterfly craft punch
- Box canvas
- Paper – patterned or plain
- Glue

Directions

1. Draw two faint pencil lines on your canvas – the lines should cross the canvas in a basic triangular shape.

2. Punch a few butterfly shapes and fold them in half. Start arranging them on the canvas within the lines that you just drew. With this picture, the fewer straight lines you have the better.

3. Glue one side of the butterfly to the canvas. Repeat for all the butterflies.

Journaling Made Easy

Materials

- An old book
- Sharpies in different colors
- Assorted patterned papers
- A fine liner pen
- Photos and photo corners
- Water color pigments
- Coarse sand paper

Directions

1. You are going to use the old book as a base for a brand new journal.

2. Start with your title page – paint it if you want, create different textures and backgrounds.

3. Draw a picture that appeals to you with the fine liner.

4. Place the sand paper underneath the page and then rub the Sharpies over it so that the texture is moved onto your page.

5. Place your photo at the center as the heart of the flower. Use photo corners to keep it in place.

6. Punch out some shapes with coordinating paper and glue them in.

7. Embellish the pages to your heart's content.

Conclusion

Thank you for downloading this book!

I really hoped that you enjoyed the projects that I've shared with you. These projects can be used a starting point for your own creative journey – feel free to mix and match techniques in a manner that appeals to you.

The one rule when it comes to crafting is that there are really no rules – anything goes.

Have fun with your crafting and good luck with your projects!

Never, ever stop creating.

For Images Of The Final Product For Each Of These Crafts Click Here

Final Words

I would like to thank you for downloading my book and I hope I have been able to help you and educate you about something new.

If you have enjoyed this book and would like to share your positive thoughts, could you please take 30 seconds of your time to go back and give me a review on my Amazon book page!

I greatly appreciate seeing these reviews because it helps me share my hard work!

Again, thank you and I wish you all the best with your crafting!

Read This FIRST - 100% FREE BONUS

Check Out Kitty's Free Giveaway!

FOR A LIMITED TIME ONLY – Get Kitty's Best Selling book "*100 Ultimate Crafts For A Rainy Day"* absolutely FREE!

<u>CLICK HERE to download YOUR free copy!</u>

Readers who have read the bonus book along with this book have seen the greatest changes in their crafting abilities and have expanded their repertoire of crafts– so it is *highly recommended* to get this bonus book.

Once again, as a big thank-you for downloading this book, I'd like to offer it to you 100% FREE for a LIMITED TIME ONLY!

<u>**CLICK HERE to download YOUR free copy!**</u>

For IMAGES of the final product of each of the crafts in this book CLICK on this link

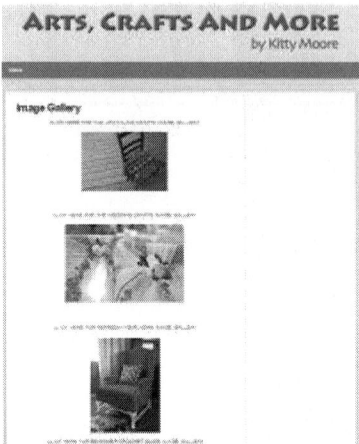

CLICK here for instant access to image gallery!

Other Books By Kitty Moore

Click Here To Check Out Kitty's Other Books!

Disclaimer

No Warranties: The authors and publishers don't guarantee or warrant the quality, accuracy, completeness, timeliness, appropriateness or suitability of the information in this book, or of any product or services referenced by this site.

The information in this site is provided on an "as is" basis and the authors and publishers make no representations or warranties of any kind with respect to this information. This site may contain inaccuracies, typographical errors, or other errors.

Liability Disclaimer: The publishers, authors, and other parties involved in the creation, production, provision of information, or delivery of this site specifically disclaim any responsibility, and shall not be held liable for any damages, claims, injuries, losses, liabilities, costs, or obligations including any direct, indirect, special, incidental, or consequences damages (collectively known as "Damages") whatsoever and howsoever caused, arising out of, or in connection with the use or misuse of the site and the information contained within it, whether such Damages arise in contract, tort, negligence, equity, statute law, or by way of other legal theory.

References

In the creation of this book, numerous sources were used in creating content.
In the creation of this book, various sources' pictures were used for demonstration purposes. The authors and publishers for this book do not hold copy right for the pictures.

The following links were used in creating this book:

http://www.allfreecrafts.com/paper/decorations/...

http://www.favecrafts.com/Papercrafts

http://www.instructables.com/id/Recycled-Magazi...

https://www.craftsy.com/project/paper-crafts?pag...

http://katiescrochetgoodies.com/2014/04/easy-ea...

Printed in Great Britain
by Amazon.co.uk, Ltd.,
Marston Gate.